DIY Free Credit Repair & Restore

Understanding & Repairing Credit the Safe and Legal Way. Know Your Rights, Delete Negative Items, 12 Step FICO Score Boosting Process in 90 Days

By

Rob Freeman

Copyright © 2017 – **Streets of Dream Press**

All Rights Reserved.

No part of this publication may be reproduced, stored in a retrieval system or transmitted in any form or by any means, electronic, mechanical, photocopying, recording or otherwise without the proper written consent of the copyright holder, except brief quotations used in a review.

Published by:

Streets of Dream Press

Streets of Dream Press
P.O. Box 966
Semmes, Alabama 36575

Cover & Interior designed

By

Jackie Bretford

First Edition

TABLE OF CONTENTS

Introduction 7
   What if you could boost your credit score quickly and with a minimum of pain? 11
   Repair you Credit Now! 12
   How to use this Book 13

Chapter 1: Getting Serious about Credit Repair: What's Holding you Back? 16
   I Started to Listen to my Self-Talk 18
   The Fear of Money is Real 20
   Fear of Complex Concepts 21
      Assess where your finances stand at the moment 23
      Now is the time to plan 23
      Talk about money 24
   Meet your New Mindset 25

Chapter 2: The Big Three: The Three Major Credit Bureaus 27
   Independent, For-Profit Companies 30
   The Credit Bureaus 32
      Equifax 33
      TransUnion 35
      Experian 36

Chapter 3: How Your Credit Score is Calculated 37
   Personal Information 38
   Public Records 39
   Credit Inquiries 39

Trade Lines 40

Bankruptcy 41

How Your Credit Score Is Calculated 42

Your Score: Five Aspects of Credit Analyzed 43

    Payment History 43

    How much Debt Do you Owe? 45

    Age of Credit History 46

    New Credit 47

    Credit Mix 48

Chapter 4: How the Lender uses this Information ... 50

    The Good News-Bad News Syndrome 51

    Charge offs 53

    Collections 54

    Late Payments 54

    Bankruptcies 55

    Foreclosures 56

    Judgments 56

Who "owns" this information? 57

    To report or not to report? That is the question. 57

    What happens when your credit is used against you? .60

Chapter 5: What It all Means 62

    Fair and Good Credit 66

The VantageScore alternative 68

    FICO scores 68

The Differences in the Scoring Formulas 70

Chapter 6: The Fair Credit Reporting Act: Your Trusted Friend 73

Who can see your Credit File..76
    Can't Misrepresent Themselves...................................82
    Prohibited Unfair Practices..83
    Garnishment...84
    What if a debt collector sues you? 86
How to Send Your Cease and Desist Letter 86
If your Debt is Sold 88

Chapter 5: The Dispute Process 90
    Obtaining Your Free Credit Report 93
        What else makes you eligible for a free report?...........95
    Who's responsible for correcting these errors? 97
    11 Quick Tips to Recognize Errors on your Report 99
    Step One..101
    If the Credit Agency Agrees 103
    If the Investigation doesn't solve the Problem 105

Chapter 6: 12 Things you can Do Right Now to Boost your Score 112
    Approach your repair plan strategically 113
    1.   Get letters of recommendation. 115
    2. Get current with any outstanding loan and credit card payments 115
    3. Negotiate..117
    4. Check your credit card limits.....................................118
    5. Obtain a secured credit card....................................119
    6. Obtain a unsecured credit card................................120
    7. Become an authorized user. 120
    8. Use your credit cards sparingly................................121

9. Ask for your credit limit to be raised 122
10. Don't close any credit cards out. 123
11. Using different types of credit 124
12. Pay your bills twice a month. 124
Conclusion 127
7 Step Checklist 129
Last words 131

INTRODUCTION

My friend, Elise, asked me to meet her at our favorite coffee shop. She sounded pretty bummed. I knew I was about ten minutes early so after getting my latte I started flipping through my smartphone.

When she walked through the door of the shop, she even sadder than she sounded on the phone. She got her coffee and wasted no time in telling me her problem.

"I tried to buy a car today," she said. "But they declined me."

I knew where this was headed, because about six months earlier I had been in her shoes.

"Why?" I asked.

"My credit wasn't good enough." She paused just long enough to take a sip of her coffee.

"I know you work at .... and you helped others fix their credit."

I nodded. I also knew where this was headed.

"Could you help me fix my credit? Please."

I know firsthand what it's like to have poor credit.

I myself suffered with it for years.

I didn't know how bad my situation was until I applied to rent an apartment and got declined. For something as simple as a place to live. That's when my situation really jumped in my face.

My first reaction was a pure and utter terror. If I couldn't get something as basic as a decent place to live, I knew something was fundamentally wrong with my finances.

That's when I changed my relationship with money and began to seriously look at my credit history. To be truthful, up until that point I didn't know my credit score, what was in my report and, quite frankly, I had little interest in any of it.

Once my credit was up to standard, I started a job a finance manager at a local car dealership, from there I moved on to a job which is consumer credit related but unfortunately I can't disclose that name here. After working 26 long years, I finally decided retire last year.

During this 28 years as a credit manager, I must say I have seen a lot, I have seen credit reports with a FICO score below 400 and I have seen scores as high as 847. But it is not always about the score, it is about how you manage your debt, it is about your LTV (loan to value) ratio. It is also about managing your credit.

8 out of 10 credit reports I saw, had errors on them, I could spot them just by taking a look, I knew if that person knew how to monitor and identify these errors, his/her score would go up another 50-100 points in just 3 months. But so many of us don't even think or worry about checking this very important report even just once a year.

I have helped some family members, friends and relatives to restore their credit. Everyone always told me I should write a book, so here it is.

One request I have before you read this, please read with an open mind and as I said there is no "ERASE" or "DELETE" button, there is no magic wand that will make all your credit blemishes disappear in a few days.
But if you follow the approach I show you here. Depending on what the items, some will disappear in 90 days, some may take 6 months and some may remain for 7 years but I promise you they will carry less weight on your score and your overall creditworthiness is vastly improve.

Lastly just so you know, when you go to buy a house, the mortgage company looks at your overall credit worthiness and not just at your FICO score. So my goal here is to improve both your overall credit worthiness and ultimately your FICO score.

So let's get started....

WHAT IF YOU COULD BOOST YOUR CREDIT SCORE QUICKLY AND WITH A MINIMUM OF PAIN?

If you believe that once your credit score takes a nosedive that's it impossible to recover from it, this book is about to change your outlook. In fact, if you allow it, this book can help you change the course of your finances and eventually your lifestyle.

What are your most cherished dreams and why are you allowing them to go up in smoke because you hold the misconception that you can't do a thing about them?

This book is what you need if . . .

. . . You have ever looked at someone who drove a good-looking, expensive car and longed for one just like it,

. . . You've ever thought about moving to the better side of town in a house with even a little more room,

. . . You've ever yearned to go back to school but didn't have the money

. . . You haven't had a vacation in years because you know you can't put any more charges on your credit card or you have no credit card to back you up financially.

REPAIR YOU CREDIT NOW!

It's time you start to think about your credit history as it stands now not as a financial death sentence chiseled in stone and more like the snapshot of the moment.

Yes, you can take your finances into your own hands and boost your score quickly.

In this book, you'll discover what your relationship to money really is and how to change it for the better. You'll learn the importance of credit bureaus, what they are and what they're not. But more than that, we'll dig in and examine your credit score, analyze where you stand. You'll also learn how your score is created – giving you deep insights into the best strategy to boost your score.

But more than that we'll take you step by step into the process of disputing any inaccuracies and errors on your report, legitimately and according to the regulations of the Fair Credit Reporting Act.

Once you learn how you can dispute the items you feel are in error on your report, you will not only help your score rise, but you'll find yourself empowered financially.

HOW TO USE THIS BOOK

This is not a book you fly through in an afternoon and toss aside or tuck into the recesses of your computer. Start by reading through the book once, without taking any actions except digesting some of the information.

After that, read through it again, this time in order to begin taking the steps outlined in this book. There's also one caveat I must make before we go any further. Don't ignore Chapter 1 that examines the fear of money. Along with that, the chapter also asks you to examine yourself to understand more fully how you got to the place you are with your credit.

Don't jump into any repair until you know that and can guarantee to yourself you're sure you're capable of making real changes.

I've written this book upon the request of my friends and family who I've helped in the past several years raise their scores so that you can be offered the terms on loans you know you can handle.

Once they experienced success following my suggestions, they've asked me, even urged me, to share my secrets to credit repair with others. Considering the extensive use of credit in the twenty-first century from cars, houses and cell phones and other expensive electronic gadgets, there's no way you can suffer from poor credit much longer.

Fixing your credit is easier than you think. It's far less painless than you fear. It's much more satisfying than you can even imagine.

It's time to stop trembling at the thought of dealing with your money and start towering over your report and your score fully in control.

Don't remain lost in the jungle of credit jargon, unable to grasp on anything that may be able to help you emerge from the darkness of low credit scores and incriminating and embarrassing credit reports.

It's time you never fear being denied credit again. It's time to pay a reasonable interest rate. It's time to take responsibility for your credit history and change it for the better.

And there's no time like the present in which to do it.

CHAPTER 1: GETTING SERIOUS ABOUT CREDIT REPAIR: WHAT'S HOLDING YOU BACK?

As I sat down with Elise to get started on repairing her credit, I asked her a few broad questions about the extent of her credit, the last time she checked her credit report as well as asking her what her credit score was.

"Oh, my goodness," she exclaimed, "I don't know any of those things. Am I supposed to know these things? Do other people know these things?"

She made a pillow from her arms and dropped her head onto them. In some odd way, she reminded me of an ostrich with her head stuck in the sand. For a moment I couldn't help myself, she reminded me of myself before told myself I had to get serious and look into my credit.

Before I owned up to my poor credit and sucked it in, I thought I had a little-known medical disorder. I simply called it "credit phobia." Regardless of how hard I tried to make friends with money and how hard I tried to pay my bills in a timely manner, I messed up over and over again.

And of course, that just created a vicious circle. The more I messed up, the more fearful I felt toward money issues, credit and my finances in general.

It felt as if I were sabotaging myself. Then one day it dawned on me. I was sabotaging myself – and I was terrified of money. Maybe fear wasn't the correct term, but I certainly began to question my "relationship" with my money.

I discovered that I was living with a limited set of beliefs that colored my views about money – not only mine but others as well.

I STARTED TO LISTEN TO MY SELF-TALK

I began listening – really listening to how I talked about those who had more money than I could ever imagine. I called them "filthy" rich. I said they had more money than they know what to do with. And I said those people usually had more money than brains.

I was setting up a mindset that soothed me. In a strange way, I felt better about not having money or credit. I certainly didn't want to be one of "those people." I couldn't possibly have enough money to live on without the fear of how I would handle it. It soon became easier to live with the fear of credit, than starting a new lifestyle, one that included I could buy just about anything I wanted.

I decided finally to Google my term "fear of credit" only to discover that a fear of financial matters really exists (who knew?). It's called Chrometophobia. The condition itself has a wide variety of symptoms, but what we really want to talk about is that whatever form your limiting beliefs of money take you must get rid of them before you can be successful in clearing your credit and keeping it clear.

The bottom line is that you must release your limiting beliefs and your fear of financial matters before you start on your quest to repair your credit. You must learn to view that you deserve good credit. Once you convince yourself of that and you clean your credit report, then you need to practice the discipline to keep your report looking financially healthy.

It's interesting to note that since I learned that term, I've discovered that there are many people who have this same fear. Several years ago British researchers conducted a study people's relationship to money. The conclusion? One out of five individuals in the United Kingdom fear money in some form. That's 25 percent! That's a lot of people who have a phobia that's seldom talked about.

Some of these individuals are so frightened of handling finances that they are unable to put any type of financial strategy into effect.

THE FEAR OF MONEY IS REAL

Here are some of the more specific results that were gleaned from that study:

Those younger than 35 years of age were more likely to fear finances than other age groups.

Women generally suffered from this fear than men.

Nearly 40 percent of those affected had no interest in personal finances.

And a whopping 45 percent – nearly half of those with this phobia – reporting racing heartbeats when faced with actually dealing with the finances.

Another 12 percent actually get physically sick when they have to deal with money.

Eleven percent feel dizziness when confronting the issue, and 15 percent are immobilized at the thought of their finances.

These statistics gave me food for thought. What causes these fears in the first place? It only seems logical if we knew what caused this irrational fear, we would then have a better idea of how to deal with it.

Some of these individuals, it seems are straddled with too much debt. Because of this, many decided to stay away from debt altogether. But avoiding the problem does little to nothing to settle the issue once and for all. It only makes the fear worse. The answer to the problem is not to stay away from money and debt, but change their attitude toward debt management.

This is probably the most important advice that you can give people living with too much debt.

FEAR OF COMPLEX CONCEPTS

While the idea of maintaining good credit isn't complex in and of itself, there are some complex issues to be confronted with you managing your debt. And these issues and financial instruments always seem to be in a continual flux.

So many of us feel as if we're continually playing "catch up" when it comes to money matters. The only way to overcome this hurdle is to learn more about the credit industry and in particular how you can work with it.

Believe it or not, you don't have to live with this fear.

I learned how to overcome and so can you. I can't emphasize this enough. It's only when you heal this fear and learn how to work with your debt, credit, and finances that you'll be able to permanently repair your credit and live the life you were meant to.

So, where do you start?

You already have taken the first step simply with your interest in doing something with your credit. Just "showing up" as they say is half the battle. Where do you go from here?

Assess where your finances stand at the moment

You may have been tossed into that spiral of poor credit and subsequent fear of finances because of even one economic disaster. It could have been a divorce, loss of employment or even life-threatening illness.

Once you know where you went off track, then you can stand back to see if that's what triggered your initial fear. Once you recognized what caused the fear in the first place will do wonders to help you overcome it and master your finances.

Now is the time to plan

If you believe that you can continue going down the financial path you have been without at least a little bit of planning, you'd be wrong. Once you've identified what caused the initial phobia – which in and of itself greatly reduces that fear – you're prepared psychologically to do some financial planning of your own.

No one achieved any goal without a minimum of a plan. That includes conquering your fear and getting back on track with your credit.

TALK ABOUT MONEY

Being closed-mouthed or secretive about your finances isn't necessarily the best move you can take. Sure, it's understandable that the entire Twitter community doesn't need to know, but you may want to talk about it to your closest family members. Just about everybody has gone through hard financial times and most people – especially those closest to you who love you – will understand.

It's absolutely essential that you talk about money, credit and finances with your spouse or you significant other if you're living with someone and sharing a checkbook. You've heard it before, but it's true: money problems are the leading cause of conflict in any relationship. If you have an otherwise satisfying and stable relationship, do not let money ruin it.

MEET YOUR NEW MINDSET

When you've taken all these steps, you'll discover that in the process you've actually changed your mindset toward money. A thought that at one time paralyzed you now only fills you with the desire to pursue your dream or change your financial plan. Either way, it will spur you to some type of action, and you'll finally discover that you, your money and your credit history can live peacefully in the same wallet.

Stop right here!

Until you know why your credit is in disarray, you shouldn't attempt any steps in this book that suggest you take out more loans, open more lines of credit or anything that potentially can get you deeper in debt.

If you do any of those things before you know how and why you are where you are now, you're not going much further with repairing your credit.

Once you've made a commitment to either overcome your fear of money or identify and analyze your past mistakes, then you can go full-steam ahead and fix your credit and create the life of your dreams.

CHAPTER 2: THE BIG THREE: THE THREE MAJOR CREDIT BUREAUS

Elise nearly choked on her coffee when I told her.

We had been meeting regularly for several weeks. Intrigued that I had boosted my credit score in a matter of three months, she confessed she had similar problems, but thought she just had to live with them until the natural term limits on them expired.

"You mean that credit bureaus aren't part of the federal government?" she asked. "Then what are they?"

What are credit bureaus, anyway?

People toss this term around like everyone knows exactly what they are.

To be honest, most individuals only have the vaguest idea of what a credit bureau is and what it does. Before you begin to boost your credit scores, though, it would be a good idea to review and get an overview of what these companies do. Knowing how they work is the key to getting any type of favorable action on your part.

Essentially, a credit bureau is a private for-profit company that makes its money by collecting and maintaining information on individuals' credit items – like yourself. It then sells this information to companies like lenders and an array of diverse creditors.

Everything that pertains to you is kept in its own file. This, of course, is referred to as your credit report. Normally, we talk about the Big Three credit bureaus, but in reality, there are literally dozens of these types of businesses scattered across the United States.

And while credit bureaus do, indeed, collect credit data, the largest of these companies do more, much more, than merely compile and report consumer credit information. You'll also learn they provide solutions for businesses in order to help them make better decisions.

They also collect and maintain items about you and your credit history, beginning from your initial credit account. They keep track of your credit history which can be a vivid picture of how dependable you are in repaying your loans.

Other information it stores on you includes the amount of credit you have at any given moment as well the amount of credit you're using and any outstanding debt collections. Of course, this in addition to any public records regarding your financial information, like bankruptcy, tax liens if you have any as well as foreclosure or any repossessions.

These agencies collect information not technically related to your credit. These data include your home address, not only your current one but also anywhere you've lived in the past. Similarly, the credit bureaus also have your employment and salary information. Some businesses find these facts and figures helpful when they're considering doing business with you.

Wait! There's still more. If all these weren't enough, these companies also provide what's called "pre-screening lists" to banks and insurance companies. These lists help the companies determine the consumers who may not only be interested – but be eligible for a certain segment of their products.

Not only that, but credit companies may buy a list of consumers who have high credit card balances. These are individuals who would be ripe and eager theoretically to transfer their balances.

INDEPENDENT, FOR-PROFIT COMPANIES

I can hear you groan now, as you say, "That's just like the big government. We have no privacy." While you may think, that given the vast range of the types of information, the government, once again, is gleefully stripping you of your privacy.

Contrary to what many individuals believe, credit bureaus are in no way connected to the federal government. They're independent, for-profit functioning databases of financial information about you and any other who has ever used credit. And in the process of collecting all of this credit history, not all of the credit bureaus will have the same information.

They collect and prepare the data, so it's in the proper format for the lender to review. This data are normally called the raw data. It's this information that is used to create a credit score. Many times persons or lenders refer to this as a FICO score. Have you ever wondered what FICO means? Actually, its real meaning is quite disappointing. It's the initials of the computer software that creates the algorithm that formulates your credit score.

There's really no surprise, given the diverse data and the number of credit bureaus that you're likely to check with all three agencies and end up with three different credit scores.

But this jumble of data and this confusing scoring of your various financial information is testimony to one thing: the importance of asking for that one free yearly credit report from each company. It's not foolproof, but it's a good start to getting a solid grasp on your credit score.

Another reason you may want to check your credit score at least yearly is to ensure that you haven't become a victim of identity theft.

Many individuals don't learn someone has stolen their vital data after most of the damage has been done.

THE CREDIT BUREAUS

Below is a little bit of history and other information on the Big Three bureaus. These facts and data give you some idea of the history of this service.

EQUIFAX

This American firm can be called the "granddaddy" of all credit bureaus. It's the largest and the oldest of the three major credit reporting agencies, or CRAs, having been established in 1899 as the Retail Credit Company.

The company experienced rapid growth right from the start. By the 1920s, the firm had offices not only throughout the United States but Canada as well. Some 40 years later, in the 1960s, the company had information on millions of Americans. The willingness of Retail Credit to distribute their information practically indiscriminately to nearly whoever requested it and paid for it, combined with their computerization of their records were two of the reasons for the passing of the Federal Fair Credit Reporting Act of 1970.

In 1975, the company changed its name to Equifax, supposedly in an attempt to improve its reputation. Today the firm gathers and maintains information on more than 800 million persons worldwide and 88 million companies and corporations across the globe.

Based in Atlanta, Georgia, this firm makes $2.7 million annually, operating in 14 separate countries. For most of its history, it had been in the business-to-business niche of the market. It also had been selling credit information and insurance reports to a diverse business customer base for many years.

Its business customers include retailers, healthcare providers, utility companies as well as government agencies as well as banks.

Equifax's mailing address is:

Equifax Information Services, LLC
P.O. Box 740256
Atlanta, Georgia 30374

This address is for general mail only. Correspondence for investigations and inquiries to your credit report as well as other matters should be mailed to the address on your latest credit report.

TransUnion

Originally established as the holding company for the Union Tank Car in 1968, the company waded into the credit industry a year later. It began by acquiring smaller regional and major city credit bureaus. The bureaus it targeted and bought usually had contracts with local retailers. Today, TransUnion has more than 250 offices in the United States and 24 offices throughout the world.

TransUnion provides both credit information and information management services to approximately 45,000 businesses as well as nearly 500 million consumers throughout the world. It's the third largest credit bureau

This corporation has evolved it credit score offering to include trended data that helps to improve the prediction odds of consumer repayment and debt behavior.

The general mailing address for TransUnion is: TransUnion, LLC

P.O. Box 1000
Chester, PA 19015

If you need to correspond with this company about an item on your credit report should be sent to the address on the report.

EXPERIAN

This company wasn't founded until 1980 in Nottingham, England. It started out as a company called CCN Systems, before entering the U.S. credit business some fifteen years later when it bought TRW Information Systems. Since then, Experian has enjoyed robust growth, with 36 offices worldwide.

Its general mailing address is:
Experian
P.O. Box 4500
Allen, Texas 75013

CHAPTER 3: HOW YOUR CREDIT SCORE IS CALCULATED

When I met Elise, she seemed to be quite perplexed. Okay. So she was downright confused and a bit irritated.

"What's wrong?" I asked her,

She shoved a bunch of papers in front of me. "I did what you said. Found out what was on my credit report. Discovered my credit score. For all the good it did me."

Indeed, I found myself holding three credit reports of varying degrees of negative items and three different credit scores."

This is probably the most frustrating and, indeed, the most daunting aspect of getting a copy of your credit reports: wading through what seems to be an indecipherable mess of paper work and the difference in scores from the various credit bureaus.

We've mentioned that each credit bureau collects different information. You'll never know how to repair your credit if you don't fully know what type of information the three major credit agencies are saying about you. For example, Equifax collects mostly information on your employment history.

PERSONAL INFORMATION

It only makes sense that each credit bureau has at least some of your personal information. This information includes your name and any version of your name you used when applying for some type of credit.

They track not only your current address but other residences you've lived in the past. They also have your Social Security number and your date of birth.

PUBLIC RECORDS

As you scan your report, you'll also discover that the bureaus gather any records on you from the courts. If you have declared bankruptcy, these bureaus will be sure to include it as well as any judgments related to your financial situation.

They'll also gather any tax liens you have against you, foreclosures and wage garnishments.

CREDIT INQUIRIES

Every time a company or an individual asks about your credit report, these credit bureaus record it. Remember the last time you stopped at that department store and filled out an application for the store's credit card? That small action was recorded with the bureaus. And just an aside at the moment, each time you do this, and someone checks your credit, it actually is considered a negative fact and can adversely affect your credit score.

TRADE LINES

These are probably the most significant part of the collection process you've never heard about. Trade lines are detailed descriptions of your loans. The credit reporting agencies not only collect the type of loan you hold and the creditor's name, but that is also who loaned you this money.

Additionally, a trade line will include the day you took the loan out as well as the last "day of activity," which means the last payment you made on it. The bureau will also have its current balance, the maximum balance of the loan and the status of the loan.

But that's not all the information these agencies have on any and all of your loans. There are usually comments written down about the loan as well as your responsibility on the account.

If you're behind on your payments, the bureaus will report that and will even record the amount past two on this transaction.

Now you may think that's all there is to report on your loan, but there's still a couple more items on each loan that you'll find in your report. You'll also discover the minimum payment due as well as the amount of the last payment you made.

BANKRUPTCY

We've mentioned earlier that the agencies will record all the public records about your financial information available in the court systems. This includes any bankruptcies you may have.

While that's correct, the details of the legal action itself is not provided by the bankruptcy court itself, but rather from third parties. The other bit of vital information you should know that some mortgage companies never actually use the word "bankruptcy," but simply use an abbreviation – "BK."

HOW YOUR CREDIT SCORE IS CALCULATED

With all this diverse information that's the CRA's have been gathering on you, you're probably wondering how they take all of this and devise a credit score. It's hard to understand how to repair your credit and improve your score when you don't have a clue on how it's calculated. If you don't know how they break down negative items or which is more damaging to you – a late payment or a wage garnishment – it's more difficult to take the proper steps to fix your credit.

750 587 **640** 500
350 **485** **835**
380 525 **599**
664
850 **631** 813 486
482

So, let's answer the first question first. How do they calculate your FICO score?

They break your score into several different areas and then assign percentages on these areas. We're going to explain the way FICO analyzes your items as it's the most popular analytic breakdown of your data.

YOUR SCORE: FIVE ASPECTS OF CREDIT ANALYZED

CREDIT SCORE FACTORS

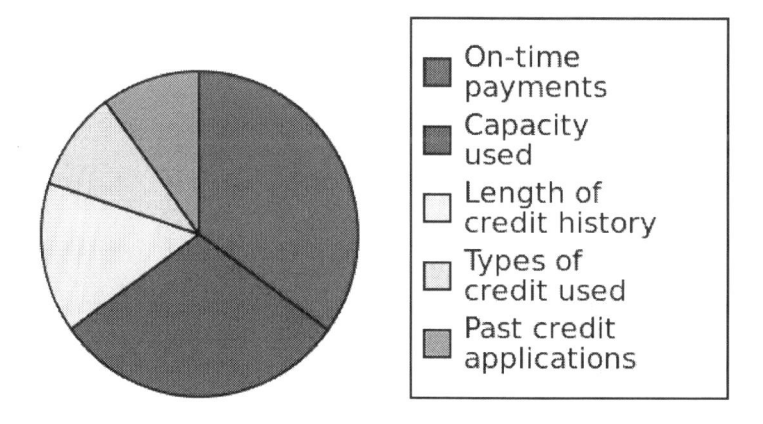

- On-time payments
- Capacity used
- Length of credit history
- Types of credit used
- Past credit applications

PAYMENT HISTORY

FICO uses five different aspects of your credit history to calculate your score. The first aspect it scrutinizes is your **payment history.** This, in fact, is the largest part of your FICO, weighing in at 35 percent of the total score.

You'll be able to recognize this history of bill payment on your report by viewing several accounts you've had for the past seven years. Listed under each identified automotive loan, mortgage and the credit card you've ever had, you'll be able to see how much you've paid per month over a longer, extended period of time instead of just how much the monthly bill was.

Then there are the cell phone carriers or even your utilities. While the companies can report your late payments and many do, they have no obligation – and typically don't – report the payments you made that were on time.

If you see that the report identifies late payments, they'll be marked not only that they were late, but how late they were, usually from 30 days to 150 days. Sometimes even more than 150 days late is noted, especially if the account went into default. As you probably suspected, the later the payment is made, the larger drop in your credit score occurs.

How much Debt Do you Owe?

The second largest category determining your credit score is your overall debt. How much do you owe? This accounts for 30 percent of your score. Remember, though, that on your report, all debt isn't created equal. An installment loan, like your house mortgage or your student loans, aren't given as much weight as other items you may owe on.

Definitely revolving debt – like credit cards – is by far a much larger segment of your overall debt. What the lenders are looking at, specifically, is what they call your debt-to-credit ratio also referred to as *credit utilization ratio*. This means they figure out the amount you owe compared to the maximum line of credit on your cards.

If you're close to maxing out your loans, then it's inevitable your credit suffers. Since this figure is a ratio, it means that two individuals with the same amount of debt could possibly have wildly divergent scores. Why would make the difference? The difference in the maximum balances and how much of the balance is available for use.

Let's say that one individual has $3,000 charged on a credit card that contains a maximum balance of $10,000 has a 30 percent debt to credit ratio. But a second consumer has the same amount charged on a card has a 60 percent ratio. How is this possible? His limit is only $5,000. You can see for yourself how much closer the second consumer is to using up the maximum amount of his limit.

AGE OF CREDIT HISTORY

The third element the CRAs use in calculating your FICO score is the age of your credit history. You might also hear this referred to as the "length" of your credit history, in either case, this category composes fifteen percent of your score. A potential lender reviewing your credit wants to know what the chances are that you're able to pay on a loan consistently over a long period of time.

The best way to show a lender you have the desire and ability to do so is by having done so already. The longer you've been paying on your loans, the better your score will be. And by the way, the more likely the potential lender will loan you the money.

The one thing missing from this category is rental payment history. Most of the time FICO scores don't include this. This is a solid method of proving your long-term dependability many times. However, a few of the credit bureaus do have a rental reporting service you can take advantage of as additional documentation when you go to apply for credit.

NEW CREDIT

The fourth element in creating your FICO score falls under the category of "new credit." On your credit report, you'll probably see it listed as "inquiries." This section refers to the number of times within the past two years you've submitted an application for credit. This can affect up to ten percent of your credit score.

Believe it or not, each time you submit an application for credit you score drops approximately five points at the beginning of that two-year period. The only exception to this is if you submitted multiple applications within a few weeks of each other for the same product. This pattern is read as you shop for a loan and is usually treated as one inquiry.

CREDIT MIX

If you've never heard of this category, it's not surprising. It's a vague category and only contributes ten percent toward your overall credit score. But that could just be the nudge your score needs to tip you into the next higher category. So, it pays for you to take a serious look at this.

Basically, the mix refers to the different types of credit you have outstanding. Lenders like to see that you use various types, not just credit cards, but personal loan and other revolving credit and installment. If you're able to do this, they feel as if loaning to you is less risky.

Now that you know how each aspect of your credit is weighed to create your score, you may want to scrutinize the report again – with a more analytic approach. It's going to be a bit easier now to see where your priorities lie when it comes to boosting that score.

CHAPTER 4: HOW THE LENDER USES THIS INFORMATION

As you can see, your credit score is a reflection of the sum total of your financial history condensed into a number. You know now that the information that the CRAs use in determining your score is all gleaned from one place: your credit report.

They ultimately use this to come to a decision if you're a good credit risk. The question the potential lender is asking is this: *If I loan this person money, what is the likelihood he'll make good on the loan and pay it off on time*? Not only that, but this score also determines what kind of interest rate you'll pay, if he does take a chance on loaning you money or issuing you a credit card.

If you've been struggling with your finances, you already know how this works. The better your score, the lower the credit rate you're charged for the loan or the card. If your credit score is low, but the lender is leaning towards granting you this, then it's possible that you'll be charged a higher interest rate when it comes to paying it back. The odds are higher that you won't be able to pay it off. So he's allowed to charge you more in credit, in order to lower any possible losses on his part.

And now we're at the crux of the situation. It's to your advantage to boost your score as much as you can. Not only will you be eligible for more loans, but in all likelihood, you'll end up saving money from the lower interest rate you can possibly get.

THE GOOD NEWS-BAD NEWS SYNDROME

Many individuals are under the impression that once their credit score plummets, they're stuck with poor credit for the rest of their lives. That's just not so. It's true that the negative information on your report that is. In fact, accurate will hang around for at least seven years. That's the bad news. However, your credit report takes the biggest hit when the negative information is new. So the negative impact fades with some with each passing year.

In contrast, though, the information on your report that is either neutral or positive usually stays there indefinitely.

All this rolls together to at least reassure you that your bad credit can't last forever if you take steps to begin to sincerely improve your credit – even if it means changing some long-held habits.

When it comes to the negative items, you still have a third alternative. That is the removal of them – at least some of them – from your report. It's not always possible, but depending on your situation it may be possible.

If you think you may try going this route, then focus on the newer negative items. As you'll recall, the newer items are more damaging to your score than the older ones. Listed below are the typical negative reports you may run into on your credit report that affects your score as well as the approximate length of time they'll stay there if you don't – or can't – get them removed.

CHARGE OFFS

If you're not familiar with the term charge-off, it refers to the action a creditor takes when he believes a debt is no longer collectible. Instead of carrying this overdue or past due debt on their books, they simply remove it from their reportable past-due accounts.

This actually helps their bottom line. By taking it off their books, the accounts receivable report improves. Don't mistake this action on the part of the creditor to mean the debt has disappeared. It hasn't. At least not from your perspective.

Your debt is then sold to a firm who pays literally pennies on the dollar for it. The intent of this purchase is to try to collect the amount owed from you. He will try to collect any court fees, interest, late charges and any other miscellaneous expenses from you.

The collector will even take the debtor to court for the full value of what's owed. Should you have a charge-off on your report, you can be stuck looking at it for up to seven years and another 180 days from the original date of delinquency.

COLLECTIONS

Another category of negative information that you may find on your credit report are known as collections. These items are a bit more complicated. Before you hurry to get these off your report, think about this. Paying them off may hurt your credit score in the long run. Why? Your repayment of these only resets the clock running on what is owed from when it was reported. Before you try to clear the collections from your report, you need to know a bit more about them.

Collection accounts can stay on your report for a maximum of seven years, just like the charge offs, from the date you first started paying late with the original creditor.

LATE PAYMENTS

Let's say you were late with a few payments on a loan, but you eventually got current with your payments. Those late payments you made? Do you think they disappeared because now you're back to paying on time? Think again.

A late payment, one that's more than a month old (30 days) can appear on the report. Some creditors won't report the first time a consumer is late, knowing that some things are just unavoidable. This is especially true if you've already established a good reputation with the lender.

They will, however, report the second incident. According to the regulations of credit reporting, once a second payment is missed, all past due payments then have to be acknowledged and reported.

Late payments or delinquent accounts legitimately reported remain for a maximum of seven years following the date of your last scheduled payment.

BANKRUPTCIES

Bankruptcies are a bit more complicated if you can believe that. First, there are two types of bankruptcies, Chapter 7 and Chapter 13. What's important to know is that this type of negative item on your report can remain on your report for more than a decade from the date you filed it. Specifically, if you filed Chapter 7, it stays on your report for ten years. Chapter 13 bankruptcies remain there for seven years.

FORECLOSURES

Again, if you've had a foreclosure, it will remain on the report for seven years. But, that doesn't mean you can't buy a house during those years this negative information is on the report. You may be able to qualify for a loan as quickly as two years after foreclosure depending on the type of loan you're getting.

JUDGMENTS

Seven years. Let's just get this up front. If you've been sued it remains as a negative item on your credit for that long. Or if the statute of limitations is shorter, it will be taken off after that has expired, whichever is longer. Most statutes of limitations are shorter than seven years.

If you have any doubts about the statute of limitations, check your state laws.

WHO "OWNS" THIS INFORMATION?

Yes, it's a strange question to ask. Who owns the information on your credit report? The surprising answer to that is the organization who had it placed on your credit report. Perhaps you would have thought the answer would have at least been the credit agency itself. But that's not the case.

The bureaus take this raw data, essentially your report and using various systems – depending on what agency it is – calculates what you ultimately see as your credit score.

TO REPORT OR NOT TO REPORT? THAT IS THE QUESTION.

We've made two points already clear. First, credit bureaus are not part of the U.S. government. They are private, for profit companies whose commodity is your financial information. While if you contemplate this for very long, you may be tempted to get a bit irritated by this arrangement. But I encourage you right now to keep a level head and deal with the problem at hand – boosting your credit score.

I realize we haven't talked much about the particular ways you can do this yet, but knowing the background of this industry (even a bit) can save you valuable time and keep you from stumbling in the dark when you go to take control of your credit.

The industry has morphed into a flourishing, profitable business. Credit agencies sell (yes, sell) your credit information to all sorts of mortgage companies, banks, automotive finance companies and any other companies that may need to know your credit score. Heck, you may even need to pay for your own credit information if you're requesting your second report within the same year.

If you're applying for a job even in which you'll be handling a large amount of money, before you're hired, the firm may tell you they're going to run a credit check on you.

You may wonder what your credit has to do with your ability to do the job. Truthfully, it doesn't. But if you have a low credit score, the company may not hire you because they would be leery you may be tempted to embezzle funds in some way in order to pay off a debt or two.

Having said all this, what you might not have known that there really is no law that requires any of these entities run your credit. And even more remarkable there is no law that demands that your creditors report your payments or any information to any of the credit agencies. All of this reporting is performed on a completely voluntary basis.

Surprised?

Most people are when they learn this. There is no law that says each of your late payments needs to be sent to the credit agencies.

If there's no law that says late payments or other derogatory information be reported to the agencies, what about the financial information that would work in your favor. There is no law that mandates this.

What happens when your credit is used against you?

Another facet of the credit industry is that the CRA's may decide to see a credit report to a legitimate inquiry that is used "against you." This means all or part of this information on file has been used to deny you a credit card, a loan, even a job. In this case, the company that has denied you the credit or job must inform you of the entity from which they received the information.

All of this information boils down to one concept: you have the right to know what's in your credit report. You're well within your rights to obtain all the information that is in your file of a credit reporting agency.

In order to do this, you need to provide the corporation with proper identification. As part of this process, you may be required to present your Social Security Number.

CHAPTER 5: WHAT IT ALL MEANS

Elise sat at our favorite coffee house waiting for me. She looked less than happy. I've been guiding her through repairing her credit. I know that she's growing increasingly more frustrated with the process.

While it's not a difficult thing to do, you do need to know a bit of the industry, the language, and some fundamental knowledge. Unfortunately, she didn't know that much.

"Look at this," Elise said, "I've got my credit scores, but I don't know what they mean. How bad are they?" she asked, "Do you know?"

Perhaps you're like our friend, Elise. You have only a passing knowledge of credit, and even though you've just received your scores, you still don't know where you stand. That's a shame, because for many of us if we just had just a bit more knowledge, we may have been able to avoid all of this in the first place.

The one thing you shouldn't do, though, is to beat yourself up over your bad credit. It happens to a lot of us. I know that bad credit crept up on me when I was younger. It was the combination of two newly acquired credit cards (back in the days when they arrived unsolicited in the mail) and shortly after that a layoff at work.

Some individuals hit a hard spot because of an illness and a pile of bills that went hand-in-hand with the poor health. Whatever the cause, it's time to take the steps to put yourself back in control of your credit.

FICO scores, as we've said before, are the most used credit rating in the country.

Most commonly these will fall within the range of 300 to 850. The higher the score, the better your rating. And you've undoubtedly discovered by now, the better the rating the more freedom you have to buy the car of your choice, your dream home and even to obtain loans and credit cards.

- 300-629: Bad credit
- 630-689: Fair credit, also called "average credit."
- 690-719: Good credit
- 720 and up: Excellent credit

According to the Fair Isaac Corporation, which created the formula to produce the credit scores, approximately 22 percent of Americans had credit scores below 600, which is commonly described as poor.

Take heart, though. Even with a score as low as 600, it doesn't mean you'll be denied every time you apply. It may be you can buy a car, but be prepared to pay more in interest than someone who even only has score tagged as fair. The lender considers you a high risk.

Of course, some lenders won't give you the time of day with a credit score like this. It's hard to predict exactly what type of loans or even the interest rate which accompanies it.

Obviously, you won't qualify for those mouth-watering no percent interest credit cards with bad credit you shouldn't hold your breath about even getting single digit interest rates.
Just about the only type of interest rate that's available to you with this credit score is what's known as "subprime" rates. These are rates that are higher than those individuals are charged who have better credit.

You may also discover that you're facing automobile and home insurance premiums and be prepared to place deposits for any utility you open in your name.

If you have poor credit right now, you may feel like you'll never be able to rise above it. It's only a natural feeling, giving the length of time it takes for accurate negative items to disappear.

But, in reality, you must remember that the credit score you hold in your hand right now is a mere snapshot of your credit activity that was taken at a specific moment in time. If you start acting as if you have a great credit right, then you'll find it rising. Just know that your score fluctuates, it changes and it changes frequently.

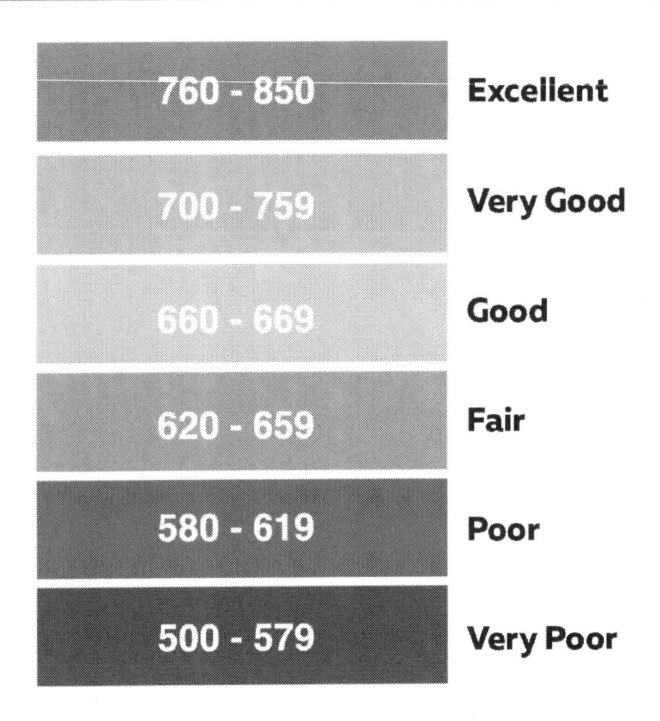

FAIR AND GOOD CREDIT

760 - 850	**Excellent**
700 - 759	**Very Good**
660 - 669	**Good**
620 - 659	**Fair**
580 - 619	**Poor**
500 - 579	**Very Poor**

As you can see from the chart, fair and good credit scores have different numbers. These two categories lie right next to each and many times consumers believe that because of the proximity on the chart, there's not much difference between how creditors treat those with fair as opposed good credit.

The truth, however, is that you can run into some big differences between the two as well as your financial opportunities in different categories.

Your largest motive for boosting your credit from fair to good comes in the form of experiencing better financial opportunities. You may still be offered loans, whether you have a fair or a good.

The real difference though lies in the interest rate that's associated with this loan. With the higher score, you'll be offered better interest rates. Similarly with a good rating as opposed to a fair one, you'll have access to more and better quality credit card offers, like better rewards, cash back and perhaps even those zero interest rates they love to dangle in your face.

If you can improve your FICO, score up to good and then beyond you'll have an easier time renting an apartment. Not only that, with a good, instead of a fair score, you should find it less stressful when your potential employer says, casually, "By the way, we're just going to run a quick credit check on you. No big deal." Right, not for them. And with good credit, not for you either.

The last thing you should do is stress over a credit score that's only rated "fair." That's not to say that you shouldn't work towards getting a good score. The point is that there may only need to be few tweaks to get your score bumped up from fair to good. The point I not to allow your score to go below what it is right now.

THE VANTAGESCORE ALTERNATIVE

FICO SCORES

The term just seems to run off your tongue. That's because until recently, it was the only game in town, as it were.

That is until the three major credit bureaus collaborated and created another scoring method beginning in 2006.

When it was first introduced, the VantageScore used an entirely different scale than FICO. Now, more than a decade later, it uses the same scale with scores ranging from 300-850.

At first, as you might imagine this new scoring technique was snubbed, being the new kid on the block. But the longer it stays around, the more the lenders are giving it a second look. Another reason it seems to have caught on is that it's widely offered to consumers without a fee.

When you first look this new scoring scale as it stands now it looks a lot like a FICO. And, indeed, they share some similarities. For example. Its top score 850 translates into better credit. The VantageScore also calculates its score using information from your credit report.

Not only that but each of the Big Three bureaus uses its own information in determining your score. This means you'll have three different scores since each agency has some differences in its reporting.

It's interesting to note that as of July 2016, this new scoring formula was used by 2,400 lenders and other credit industry participants. Not only that, but out of the 25 largest financial institutions, a whopping 20 had used it. That totaled to approximately 8 billion scores which were based on VantageScore. And that represents a near 40 percent rise in use from the year before.

Not only that, but this formula isn't done morphing and molding into a slightly different and hopefully even better snapshot at your credit. Within the next year or so, a 4.0 version will be unveiled with plans for it to be in use by 2018.

Word has it that it will rely less on your negative information, like tax liens and civil judgments that have been pulled from the public records. It's rumored that the scoring will actually differentiate medical bills from others with the intention of to treat these a bit more leniently.

THE DIFFERENCES IN THE SCORING FORMULAS

For all that's similar in these two methods of calculating your credit score, the two of these aren't without their difference.

The first difference you'll notice is that if your credit history is short, then the odds are that you'll at least have a VantageScore. Why? Because this newer formula uses "alternative data" and searches back 24 months or two years for credit activity. This compares to the six to eight months that FICO combs through.

Another difference is that the VantageScore does not take paid collection accounts into consideration. These can make a large difference in most FICO scores. According to those individuals adjusting the scoring claim that paid collection has no effect on your standing as a credit risk.

If you have one in your credit history that can make a big difference in most types of FICO scores. VantageScore says paid collections have little or no effect on how much of a credit risk you are. Another advantage to VantageScore is that it takes into account your good record on recurring payments like rent and utilities.

The newer scoring plan weighs late mortgage payments more heavily than the others. When it comes to "credit shopping" the VantageScore only takes into account a period of two weeks. Multiple credit inquiries within this time period will be considered as one inquiry. Those reviewing your record naturally presume you're looking to get credit for a loan for a car or house or some other reason. FICO, as it stands now, gives you 45 days of credit shopping clustered together.

CHAPTER 6: THE FAIR CREDIT REPORTING ACT: YOUR TRUSTED FRIEND

"I can't believe it," Elise said to me during one of our weekly meetings on your credit-repair project. *You can't be serious? Wow, all you need is an item here or there for it to spell financial death for you."*

"I agree and think how you would feel if you found mistakes on your report, and no one had to fix them. You had to live with them for at least seven years."

"It could ruin you financially," Elise agreed. *"I'm not exaggerating the situation either."*

At the beginning of the twentieth century, the credit industry was growing incredibly fast. There were any number of small regional credit bureaus gathering information on consumers for the sole purpose of selling these data to potential lenders

It's surprising then that it took nearly 50 years before Congress created the first piece of legislation regulating the industry while protecting the rights of consumers. Prior to this consumers had no recourse should there be any errors on your credit report.

Specifically, the FCRA spells out your rights if, based on the facts in your credit report, a lender denies you credit or a potential employer refuses to hire you.

The act, in a nutshell, specifies that if a company takes any adverse action based on the facts on your credit report, it must provide you with the following information: the name, address, and Telephone Company that provided them the report.

Of course, the law states that you show proper identification in order to receive this. This could take the form of your Social Security number. The act states that, in addition to this situation, there are several other scenarios that could including any other adverse action occurred to the information in your file, or your identity stolen. Should you be a victim of this last scenario, you have the right to have what's called a fraud report include in your information.

Other reasons which may prompt a free report if it's inaccurate because of any type of fraud or if you're on public assistance. If you're currently unemployed or looking for a job within 60 days, you're also eligible for a free report.

All of this, of course, is in addition to the free yearly report that's due to you, not only from the Big Three credit bureaus but also from the lesser, more specialized reporting firms as well, such as those that deal solely with check writing history.

The FCRA grants you the right to know your credit score as well. These scores, by the way, aren't automatically put on your report. You have to receive these separately.

The national act made it clear that each consumer had a right to be aware of the information on your report. Today, you can find your credit score for free from a variety of sites on the web.

And that brings us to the nuts and bolts of the legislation: your right to challenge the veracity of the data on your report. As you're well aware, this applies to any inaccuracies. But you might not be aware that the FCRA ensures that any incomplete data be challenged and ultimately removed if it can't be revised to reflect an accurate score.

Not only that, but the information must be erased from your report within 30 days of being first notified of the potential errors.

As you already know, negative items can only remain on your report for seven years – no longer. Thereafter, it's your fundamental right to have any outdated items removed as well. Should you find an item older than seven years, for example, you need to contact the reporting agency.

WHO CAN SEE YOUR CREDIT FILE

The reporting agencies are by law only allowed to show this information about you with those who a valid need. These entities include, but might not be limited to those with whom you've applied for credit or insurance companies that you had dealings with, landlords and potential employers.

By the way, it's at the discretion of the reporting agency who actually requires this information. The bottom line though is that no one can get a copy of your report without your full consent.

A credit agency can't even give your report to your current or any potential employer without your knowledge and your written consent. The only exception to this is the trucking industry, where your written consent is not required.

If you receive "prescreened" offers for credit cards and insurance, and you'd rather not, the CRA also addresses that as well. It provides you with the right to have your name removed from the mailing list. The companies providing you with these offers are mandated to provide you with their toll-free telephone number in order to contact them and inform them of that. Your other course of action is to call **1.888.5OPTOUT or 1.888.567.8688.**

You might not be aware of this, but you're entitled to seek damages if any of your rights have been violated.

The Fair Credit Reporting Act, as groundbreaking as it was when it was enacted in 1970 soon proved to help the state of the credit industry in addition to protecting your rights.

That's why it's so puzzling that it took nearly another decade to create, pass and implement a bill that restraints certain actions the debt collections community, also known generically as "bill collectors."

In 1977, Congress passed the Fair Debt Collections Practices Act. A long winded name for a law that places limits on methods of debt collections. Specifically, it outlaws the use of abusive, unfair or deceptive practices in order to strong-arm you to pay the debt.

The law defines a debt collector as a company that buys delinquent debts in order to collect on them.

The act covers any personal debts, household, and family debts. Those are defined as any outstanding balance on a personal credit card, automobile loans as well as medical bills and, of course, the mortgage on your house.

You should note that this piece of legislation does not apply to business debts.

One of the most important results of the bill is that it sets limits on the hours of the day anyone seeking payment may call you. They can only call you between the hours of 8 a.m. and 9 p.m. unless they have your permission to call at other hours. They're allowed to call you at work unless you tell them otherwise. Once they're aware they aren't supposed to call you at work, then they must abide by this.

In fact, these individuals can use any method to reach out to you – even e-mail unless otherwise requested – as long as they specifically tell you they are contacting with the express intent to collect a debt and they don't pose as someone they're not such as an attorney or an official from a government agency.

Believe it or not, you don't have to tolerate the continual calling of these individuals. If you wish them to stop calling you, simply send them a letter and inform them. At the end of the chapter for this purpose. Feel free to use it.

If you've hired a lawyer to deal with this issue, then they can't call you, but must go through your attorney.

What if they are calling others about you? Is this legal?

It is, as a matter of fact, but they can only contact a person once and the only thing they may ask him is your current address and telephone number. They can't talk about the debt itself unless he is speaking with your spouse or your attorney.

Here's a little-known part of this act that may serve you well in the long run. You are entitled to a written validation of the debt the individual is called you about. What's more, you must receive this within five days of his initial contact. This should be done automatically from his firm. You don't have to request it. This is called a validation letter.

The purpose of this letter is to inform you the exact amount of the debt, as well as your next steps if you believe you don't owe this money. Now, you would think these scenarios would cover just about anything you could possibly encounter.

Almost, but not quite.

Here are a few more steps they can never (repeat never) take when trying to collect a debt.

Let's start with harassment. Specifically, the law says they can't harass, oppress or abuse you in any way as part of the attempt to collect the debt. Harassment covers a wide range of actions. For example, it can be considered harassment if they threaten to do you harm or to resort to violence or publish a list of those individuals who have refused to pay their legal, financial obligations.

CAN'T MISREPRESENT THEMSELVES

Collection agents are not allowed to intentionally lie to you. They can't claim you've committed crimes when you haven't nor can they "misrepresent" the amount of money due. They can't contend they're sending you legal forms if they aren't legal forms. In other words, they can't coerce you into paying by presenting information as if were legal documents.

They also can't tell you the forms they're sending are legally binding documents when they really are.

There are several actions that this act protects you from. They are prevented by this law from threats that you'll be arrested if you don't pay. These companies have no power to seize your money through garnishment, attachment or through the sale of your personal property unless they're permitted by law. In other words, they can't say these things as scare tactics in order to get you to pay under duress.

Nor can they contact you using a false company name. They have to be, from the moment, they're on the phone, upfront with you about who they are.

Prohibited Unfair Practices

The act outlines a few of the "unfair practices" debt collectors used to do in order to strong arm you into paying. These companies or individuals can't attempt to collect interest, free or other various charges in addition to the delinquent account unless the contract that created your debt allows this.

They can't deposit a post-dated check early. They must abide by the date on the check. If you owe money on more than one debt he/she is collecting; it's at your discretion which debt you want to apply your payment to at first. But even more importantly, he/she can't apply your payment to a debt you don't believe you owe.

Garnishment

Garnishment is a serious action in an attempt to collect a debt. It's going through your employer to deduct the payments from your paycheck even before it's issued to you. While garnishment is perfectly legal and many individuals experience this each year, the collection agent can't just take this action on their own.

The collection agency must take you to court for the permission. If they do get permission, you'll be issued a judgment. There are, however, certain types of income that can't be garnished, including Social Security benefits, Supplemental Security Income, Veterans' benefits, Civil Service and Federal Retirement and Disability benefits, Military annuities and Survivors benefits, Federal Emergency Management Agency Federal Disaster Assistance.

The only way any of these types of income can be garnished is to pay for back payments of child support, delinquent taxes, alimony, or student loans.

Now, you may be thinking that's all well and good, but exactly what's the use even knowing this if I can't do something on my behalf should any of these circumstances occur.

Ahh, but there's where you're wrong. The law also outlines what you can do on your behalf. First, you should know that you have a legal right to sue the collection agency in either a state or federal court within a year of the violation.

Should you win, then the collector is obligated to pay for damages you incurred due to their illegal activities. These items could include lost wages and medical bills. Additionally, the court may also award you $1,000 in reimbursement regardless if you can prove you suffered damage or not. And of course, if you win, you'll be reimbursed your court costs and attorney fees.

WHAT IF A DEBT COLLECTOR SUES YOU?

If that should occur, then you or your attorney should respond to the lawsuit by the date specified on the documents you receive.

Keep in mind that you have the right to request the collection agent to stop contacting you. Merely write a letter that makes this request. Then send it by certified mail to the address you have on any correspondence you have had with them. Once they receive this letter, they must abide by it.

They may legally contact you after this to inform you that they won't contact you anymore (yes, the law states that.) or to inform you if they are taking a specific action against you, such as filing a lawsuit.

HOW TO SEND YOUR CEASE AND DESIST LETTER

Type this letter into your computer and make a folder to save it or save it in the same file you have other credit-related materials. Print it out. Then, send your letter via certified mail, 'return receipt requested' to the collector.

If you're not sure how to send a piece of mail in this manner, simply take the letter to your local post office. They can show you how to do it. When you send it in this fashion, you'll be able to track the letter to ensure the debt collection agency received it. As with all your correspondence regarding your credit history retain a copy of the letter for your own records.

Date

Your Name
Address
City, State Zip

Debt Collector's Name
Address
City, State Zip

Re: Account Number

Dear Debt Collector:

According to my rights under Federal Debt Collection laws, I'm requesting that you cease and desist all forms of communication with me, as well as my family and friends, in relation to this and all other alleged debts you claim I owe.

You are hereby notified that if you do not comply with this request, I will file a complaint with the Federal Trade Commission and the [your state here] Attorney General's office. Civil and criminal claims will be pursued.

Sincerely,

Your Name

IF YOUR DEBT IS SOLD . . .

You can only send this cease-and-desist letter to third-party debt collectors. These are collectors who have brought your account from the original owner. And it only applies to the company that owns it at that time.

It's not uncommon for debts like yours to be sold more than once in an attempt to get the debtors to pay. Let's say your debt was owned by ABC Corporation when you sent the letter. They bought your debt from the original owner.

Should ABC Corporation, for whatever reason, decides to sell this debt – as part of a package of a group of accounts – to XYZ Corporation. The XYZ Company then begins to call you about making arrangements to pay. The cease-and-letter you for ABC doesn't apply for the new company. You must send a letter to XYZ for them to stop calling you.

CHAPTER 5: THE DISPUTE PROCESS

"I sent my first dispute letter out today," Elise told me at one of our weekly meetings.

"Good," I answered. She had come a long way in regards to her relationship with her credit since we've been meeting on a weekly basis.

"How do you feel about that?" I asked her even though I think I knew the answer from her smile.

"Empowered," she said. "Empowered and for the first time in a long time, hopeful."

That's what many people say once they start seriously grappling with their bad credit.

Empowered. Hopeful.

And it can be how you feel as well, once you start the actual dispute process.

With the credit industry growing fast and furious during post-World War II into the late twentieth century – and even up to today – it's little wonder that there are inaccuracies on your credit report.

In fact, there's another growing problem that nearly mandates we all review our credit regularly is identify theft. With online shopping and the burgeoning of technology, it's easier than ever for someone to take your identify and go on a shopping spree without the worry of the consequences of a ruined credit history.

Add in the seriousness of the information the credit bureaus handle day in and day out; you'd think the industry would be extremely careful with what goes on your report.

You would think so.

But the truth is that one out of four consumers has found errors on their credit report. When I received my credit report and reviewed it, I discovered someone else's bankruptcy was placed in with my information.

Of course, it was an honest mistake. After all, what are the odds of two people living on the same street with the same first and last name (the only difference in our names were our middle names)?

The bottom line is that mistakes and errors show up on these reports more than anyone would care to admit. And there's no one but yourself that has the power to correct them.

If you're not vigilant about reviewing your credit report yearly, you may be in for a less than pleasant surprise when you apply for a loan, a car, or even your dream home.

Today, thanks to the Fair Credit Reporting Acts and other related legislation, you have a right to make the bureaus correct the errors.

OBTAINING YOUR FREE CREDIT REPORT

In order to obtain you're a free copy of your credit report, all you need to do is ask for it. An amendment to the Fair Credit Reporting Act mandates that the Big Three credit bureaus, provide you with a copy at your request every twelve months.

In order to facilitate these requests, the credit bureau have worked together and created a website where consumers, like yourself can request this copy. The site is annualcreditrepport.com.

You can also request a copy of your report by calling this number **1.877.322.8228**. If you'd rather put your request in writing simply complete the Annual Credit Report Request Form found on the web, print it out and mail it to:

Annual Credit Report Request Service
P. O. Box 105281
Atlanta, GA 30348-5281

If you try to contact the three nationwide credit reporting companies, they will simply refer you to these sites:

Equifax Credit Reporting Agency

https://www.equifax.com/personal/

TransUnion Credit Reporting Agency

https://www.transunion.com/

Experian Credit Reporting Agency

http://www.experian.com/

When you contact this website or call them, you'll be able to order all three of your reports, one from each of the major credit bureaus at the same time, but you don't have to. If you only want one or two of them, they can accommodate you

Be prepared to provide the following information: Your name, Social Security number and your date of birth. You may be asked to provide your previous address if you've within the past two years.

There is one last thing; the company may ask you a personal question that no one else would know, like the amount of your car payment. If you're ordering three free ones – one from each credit bureau --, you shouldn't be surprised (or get irritated) if they ask you three separate security questions, one for each of the copies, which, of course, are coming from three different sources.

WHAT ELSE MAKES YOU ELIGIBLE FOR A FREE REPORT?

You can also receive a free report if you're denied credit or a firm's services based on a review of your report. These incidents include, but aren't limited to adverse actions like denying your application for credit or refusing to provide you with insurance or even with failing to hire you based on the facts in the report.

The company must put this in writing and will give you the name, address, and the telephone number of the credit reporting agency the firm used to evaluate you. There is one catch though. Once you receive the written notice of denial, you have 60 days to request your free copy.

You're due a free copy of your information if you've been unemployed and plan to search for work within sixty days, if you're on government assistance or if your report is inaccurate because you've had your identify stolen or you've been the victim of fraud.

What if you need a second copy of your report before the twelve-month period is up? Of course, you can receive one, but you'll have to purchase it for a nominal fee. To purchase a copy of this report call the separate bureaus at the following telephone numbers or visit their websites:

Experian-1.888.397.3742
www.experian.com

TransUnion-1-800-916-8800
www.transunion.com

Equifax-1.800.685.1111
www.equifax.com

WHO'S RESPONSIBLE FOR CORRECTING THESE ERRORS?

The parties responsible for correcting these reports and then adjusting the reports lie with both the credit bureaus as well as the corporation that provided that piece of information to the bureau. In order to use all of your rights under the Fair Credit Reporting Act.

Warning: From this moment on in the dispute process you are now exiting the internet zone.

That's right! Whatever correspondence or contact you have from here on with the credit bureaus, you must do so through the mail. And I don't mean email. The only way to contact the credit bureaus to request either correction of items or if you want something removed completely is through the United States Postal Service. What's more, you should send nothing to any of these bureaus without sending it certified mail, return receipt requested.

Now that you've got your copy of your credit report, carefully study it. You know enough by now to understand how your credit number is scored and weighted that you now know where to start studying your raw data.

11 QUICK TIPS TO RECOGNIZE ERRORS ON YOUR REPORT

As we mentioned before, an "error" on your credit report isn't restricted to the debt itself. Any information associated with the entry, from a mistake in your name to inaccurate payment dates can qualify as a disputable error.

The following are a few reminders on how to recognize an error on a credit item.

The first category of errors deal with the account itself and could include: a late payment that was made more than seven years ago. That's old news and should not be on your report.

- A credit card or loan listed on your report that isn't yours, you're not co-signer for or an authorized user on.

- An account you closed, but the report attributes the closing to the provider.

- A legitimate error for which you're eligible to file a dispute comes under the "derogatory remarks" category. Classic examples of these include:

- A collections account which you have already paid off is showing that it isn't paid off yet.

- A tax lien older than seven years

- An account discharged in a bankruptcy that shows up on the report with an active balance.
- If any of the personal information is wrong – even if the account data is accurate – can be disputed as well. What kind of information should you check and double check?

- Your name isn't listed correctly.

- An address at which either have never lived or used as a mailing address.

- Showing employment history that's inaccurate.

- You need to realize that when you dispute the personal information, the results are not likely to affect your credit score. But mistakes here could be a good early harbinger of possible fraud.

STEP ONE

Inform the credit reporting agency, through a written, formal business letter, what data in your report is erroneous. And don't worry. At the end of this chapter is a sample letter that I encourage you to use, word for word, for this purpose. I've left blanks so you can plug in the data that's wrong. But the letter is ready to use and is already formatted in the form of business correspondence. All you need to do is type it up and print it out.

Be sure to include in this letter all copies of the documents that support your argument. Never send original documents. You keep those safe with you. Just make copies of the data you intend to send them.

Of course, your letter will include your complete name and address. Then identify those documents you're providing the credit agency. State, as clearly as you can, why you're challenging the information and make it as plain as you can that you would like these data to be removed or corrected.

It's wise to send a copy of your credit report with the items you're referring to either highlighted or circled. This ensures the person reviewing it has some guidance in finding them.

Once you've covered all the items you believe are wrong, then put all this information in an envelope and take it to the Post Office. You're going to request that it be sent by certified mail, "return receipt requested."

This means that when your correspondence reaches the credit agency, someone must sign for it. And when they do, you'll get a copy of a receipt that the data had reached its destination.

By the way, you may either mark that date on a calendar or display the receipt somewhere you can see it or both. The moment someone has signed for the letter, the clock starts ticking.

Oh, yeah. It does.

By law, the companies have 30 days in which to review the disputed items and provide you with an answer. In addition, though, the credit agency is required to forward all relevant material to your dispute to the specific organization from which it received that information.

When you send disputed items only send one item per envelope and letter. If you find three inaccuracies in your report, then you'll need to send three separate letters indicating what's incorrect, using three separate mailing envelopes.

In this way, you're assured each item is getting the attention it deserves and the bureaus can't say they didn't see one hidden in the stack you gave them.

IF THE CREDIT AGENCY AGREES

If the credit reporting agency agrees and discovers that the information you've brought to their attention is, indeed, inaccurate and needs to be revised, its responsibilities don't end there. It's then required to notify the Big Three credit bureaus. Once those companies receive that they then they must correct the information in their file. In this way, the odds are less likely that the misinformation will be passed around again.

Once the inquiry has been settled, then the credit reporting agency must provide you with the results *in writing as well as a free copy of the credit report with the revisions made.*
The report you receive with the resolution of this inquiry doesn't count as your free copy for the year. So, when the time arrives, you can receive another free copy.

But, wait. You're still protected in another way. The credit reporting agency is barred from placing that disputed information back on your report unless the company that provided the data originally can prove it really is accurate. Not only that but, the credit reporting company also must send you data on the agency which originally placed the erroneous information on the report.

Upon your request, the company which originally made the errors must send notices of any corrections to anyone who read your report in the past six months. You can also go one step further than that by having a corrected copy of the report sent to any firm which during the last years received the inaccurate one and was reviewing data and ma

If you ask, the credit reporting company must send notices of any corrections to anyone who received your report in the past six months. You can have a corrected copy of your report sent to anyone who received a copy during the past two years for employment purposes.

IF THE INVESTIGATION DOESN'T SOLVE THE PROBLEM

What happens should the dispute isn't resolved?

You still have legal recourse. This approach won't take the item off your report, but it will let potential creditors know that you have disputed its accuracy. You can request that a statement of the dispute be included in the file as well as future reports.

You can also request the credit agency to provide your statement to all who received a copy of your report in the recent past. But be prepared, if you do this, you'll have to pay for it.

While you're doing all of the above, you may think that your work is done.

Wrong!

You also need to send a letter to the person, firm or organization that provided the credit bureau with this information originally. Again, it needs to be a certified letter with receipt requested so you know when the provider received the letter.

Inform this company that you are disputing an item in your report. At the end of the chapter we've provided a sample letter that you can use. Again, you'll send copies, not originals, of all the documents you believe build your case.

If the provider has included an address on your report, then mail this information to that address. If there is no address, contact the provider through other means and request their address. But again, it's imperative you don't use the internet as a way to challenge the accuracy of this report.

If he doesn't give you a specific address to send this material, you can use any business address you find for this firm.

If the provider chooses to ignore you and continues to report this item then to the credit bureau, then it must also let the credit reporting agency know that you have disputed it to them, the provider.

If you're correct and the material they're reporting is, indeed wrong or even incomplete, then the provider must inform the credit agency of this development.

Letter to Credit Bureau

Date
Your Name
Your Address
Your City, State, Zip Code

Complaint Department
Name of Credit Bureau
Address
City, State, Zip Code

Dear Sir or Madam:

I am writing to dispute the following information in my file. The items I dispute also are encircled on the attached copy of the report I received.

This item (identify item(s) disputed by name of source, such as creditors or tax court, and identify type of item, such as credit account, judgment, etc.) is (inaccurate or incomplete) because (describe what is inaccurate or incomplete and why). I am requesting that the item be deleted (or request another specific change) to correct the information.

Enclosed are copies of (use this sentence if applicable and describe any enclosed documentation, such as payment records, court documents) supporting my position. Please reinvestigate this (these) matter(s) and (delete or correct) the disputed item(s) as soon as possible.

Sincerely,

Your name [your signature and then your name printed below it]

Enclosures: (List what you are enclosing)

Letter to the company that provided credit bureau with inaccurate information

[Your Name]
[Your Address]
[Your City, State, Zip Code]
[Date]

Complaint Department

[Company Name]
[Street Address]
[City, State, Zip Code]

I am writing to dispute the following information that your company provided to **[give the name of the credit reporting company whose report has incorrect information]**. I have circled the items I dispute on the attached copy of the credit report I received.

This **item [identify item(s) disputed by type of item, such as credit account, judgment, etc., and your account number or another method for the information provider to locate your account]** is **[inaccurate or incomplete]** because **[describe what is inaccurate or incomplete and why]**. I am requesting that **[name of company]** have the item(s) removed **[or

request another specific change] to correct the information.

Enclosed are copies of **[use this sentence if applicable and describe any enclosed documents, such as payment records and court documents]** supporting my position. Please reinvestigate this [these] matter[s] and contact the national credit reporting companies to which you provided this information to have them**[delete or correct]** the disputed item[s] as soon as possible.

Sincerely,

Your name

Enclosures: **[List what you are enclosing.]**

CHAPTER 6: 12 THINGS YOU CAN DO RIGHT NOW TO BOOST YOUR SCORE

Elise just threw up her hands. "I'll be 92 years old before I could even begin to clean up this mess," she said her eyes downcast. "Isn't there anything I can do right now that might make even a smidgen of a difference? Something that would bring up my score by a couple of points at least."

Stop!

Once you have a copy of your credit score, you may be tempted to jump in and begin trying to make adjustments everywhere. Resist that temptation. Resist it with every muscle in your body. After all, like our friend Elise in the paragraph above, you'd like nothing more than to wave a magic wand over your report and announced loudly, "Abracadabra! Money worries, be gone!"

APPROACH YOUR REPAIR PLAN STRATEGICALLY

If you simply jump in and try to do everything you think needs done from that first glance of your report, you may be doing more damage than good. Just step back for a moment and think about it.

You know, for example, that 35 percent of your credit score is a reflection of your payment history. That's the largest chunk of your report. This means even one late payment can deflate that score quickly.

And this is where you can begin today to improve this portion of your score. No, you can't just indiscriminately ask the companies to remove items – especially if there is no error. But, what you can do is to begin to establish a positive history.

If you're serious about boosting your credit score, then you need to give some serious thought about why in the past you paid some of these items late. Was it lack of money, medical emergencies or the irresponsible actions of a younger version of you? Vow right now, that from this moment you'll make all your payments on time. Do you have a house payment? Ever paid it late? Make it a priority to pay it on time. The same thing goes for any car payments you may have. Push these bills to the top of the priority list on payday.

Make sure these bills are paid on time, even if you have to take money out of two or more paychecks. Make sure these bills are paid, even if you need to adjust your budget. You made need to allocate a little less money for entertainment or even take a few dollars out of the grocery fund.

You get the idea; these are just two types of bills that cannot be paid late. Not if you're trying to raise your credit score.

1. GET LETTERS OF RECOMMENDATION.

This is also going to be your mantra for all of your utility bills or if you open any new credit cards – either secured or unsecured. No, you're right utility bills are not normally listed on credit reports – and certainly not if you've been paying them off faithfully for years.

But there's no reason if you've been a good customer – one for several years with no late payments – to ask that firm for a recommendation to present to the company you're requesting a loan.

2. GET CURRENT WITH ANY OUTSTANDING LOAN AND CREDIT CARD PAYMENTS

If your financial situation still has you strapped to making late payments, turn this around as quickly as possible. Get caught up with any payments you've been behind on – from your house payment to your car payments, credit card balances and student loans.

Once you're making your payments in a timely fashion, you'll be surprised how quickly your score will begin to rise. Not only that, but you'll begin to have more confidence in your ability to raise your score.

If you believe that getting current with your credit cards will take longer than you like, then contact your credit card, holders. Ask them if there is any way they can hammer out a payment plan that they would accept as a current lower payment. If you've been even a fairly good customer, the credit card company will try to work with you.

Once you begin meeting the new terms, then these companies won't be reporting your payments as late. And in the process, you'll get some breathing space to get your act together in other areas of your finances.

Even some car finance companies are willing to offer you a deal sometimes. They will defer a payment that obviously is late to the end of your loan. But be careful when you do this, sometimes there's a penalty for being late again — a steep penalty. But it's at least worth checking it out, so you have a better grasp of your options.

3. NEGOTIATE

This is no time to be shy. Now, in fact, is the perfect time to practice your assertiveness. Let's say that one of the negative items on your credit report is a period of time when you stopped paying your credit card bill during an extended period of unemployment.

That doesn't mean, however, that there's nothing you can do. Reach out to these creditors. Ask if they could "erase" that debt or, for that matter, any account that went into collection. Make an offer to pay the remaining balance if the creditor would report the account as "paid as agreed." You may even be able to get this splotch on your credit removed completely.

The only caveat in this approach is that you ensure the creditor puts this agreement in writing before you make your payment.

Another similar path you may want to take to get to the same place is to ask for what's known as a "good-will adjustment." Let's say you were a good customer on your Visa or Master Card until you hit that bump of unemployment. Ask the credit card company to have the late payments during that period removed from your report. Of course, you'll want to do this in writing. This has been known to happen and is certainly worth a try.

4. CHECK YOUR CREDIT CARD LIMITS

This may seem like a simple and obvious action to take – especially after you've learned that the closer you are to approaching the maximum limit on the credit card the more, it adversely affects your score. Ensure that your reported credit limits are current. If the report shows a lower limit than what you really have could bring down that score. If it's wrong on your report – lower than what you currently have – ask the credit card company to report your higher limit.

5. OBTAIN A SECURED CREDIT CARD

A secured credit card is one in which the credit limit is backed by money you've paid the credit card company to use in case you fail to make your monthly payments. Let's say you pay the credit card company $500. The card company issues you a card with a $500 credit limit.

Your responsibility is to at least pay the minimum balance every month. The card company is to report your payment to the credit bureau. What happens if you default in some form? That's why the credit card company or bank is holding your $500. It keeps at least some portion of it. Now you see how this is a great no-risk move to the company.

If on the other hand, you make your payments on hand, you may have two options. The first is to offer to put even more money in an account to back up your card which in turn gives you a larger credit limit.

Or it may be time to take the next step as indicated below.

6. OBTAIN A UNSECURED CREDIT CARD

This is the conventional card. Don't expect a huge credit limit at first, but just the fact that you have an unsecured card is a good step. You have to ensure, though, that you don't skip a payment and you don't use the maximum credit limit. This step alone goes a long way to boosting your credit score.

7. BECOME AN AUTHORIZED USER.

Can't get a traditional card and don't have the money for a secured one? There's still one more option yet. Become an authorized user on another person's card. If you can convince a relative or close friend to add you to their already existing account, you can experience several benefits.

Make sure that you and the owner of the card have a written agreement explaining how much you can spend every month and how you'll pay your share back to him.

The benefit? Every time your friend pays his card (which includes your portion of the spending), it will appear on your report as well, since you're identified as an authorized user. In this way, you're building a positive credit history.

8. USE YOUR CREDIT CARDS SPARINGLY

Welcome to the paradoxical world of credit.

Yes, you're absolutely right. I did spend quite a bit of time explaining several different ways for you to obtain credit cards, because, quite frankly, a good payment record on them is that important.

Now that it seems like you went through this trouble to get a few, you're told not to use them? Well, not exactly, but that's a close summary of the situation. The key is that as I've said before you want to keep the ratio between your credit and what you actually use, which incidentally is called the "credit utilization ratio" to 30 percent.

Of credit experts tell you that if you keep it to 10 percent ($1,000 limit with only $100 used for example), that's even better. That seems to be the ratio that will maximize this portion of your FICO score.

9. ASK FOR YOUR CREDIT LIMIT TO BE RAISED

If you can't hit that golden mean ratio one way, then meet it the other way.

Call your creditors to see if there isn't some possible way they could raise your credit limit to get you closer to the 30 percent or even 10 percent credit utilization ratio.

If they agree, then you have to keep in mind the ultimate reason you did this: to obtain a more favorable credit ratio. So, rein in that temptation to spend more "just because you can." Before you know it, you'll find yourself right where you started from.

10. DON'T CLOSE ANY CREDIT CARDS OUT.

Now, this is a piece of advice that doesn't make any sense on the surface. But if you cancel a card it will only cause your available credit to plummet. This becomes a negative spot on your credit.

Instead of closing it out, why not make this a "dedicated" credit card. You can use it, for example, to only pay recurring charges, like a utility bill.

11. USING DIFFERENT TYPES OF CREDIT

This is another one of those suggestions to implement only if you're sure you can repay the loan. Credit bureaus like to see different types credit on the report for different reasons. If you recall, ten percent of your FICO score is based on that category referred to as "credit mix." You may want to buy a piece of furniture or even an appliance with an installment loan from a credit union.

Here again, if this is part of your strategic approach to improving your credit, just make sure you can follow through on this and pay off the loan. Otherwise . . . you're only digging yourself into a deeper hole.

12. PAY YOUR BILLS TWICE A MONTH.

What? This won't necessarily apply every month. But we've all experienced a month that looked a lot like

Murphy's Law -- what can go wrong will go wrong. When this occurs, there's no way around not using your credit. And this doesn't leave a positive mark. So if you've had to rely on credit to see you through one month here's what you do . . .

Take a look at this example of what happened to my friend. His credit limit was $3,000. But as the month of Murphy's Law raged on, he discovered he needed to use $2,900 of that for doctor's visits, car repair and an airline ticket for his son who was headed to college.

And of course, he had every intention of paying it all off at one time.

But until then, he knew it would stick out like a sore thumb on his credit report. So, he made one payment right before the statement closing date. Then he made a second payment right before the due date. This was a good move. His first payment more than likely reduced the balance the credit bureaus saw, giving him a good ration of what he owes to his maximum balance.

He doesn't look like he's gone crazy maxing out his credit card. The second payment ensured he would pay no interest or late fee.

CONCLUSION

Elise was bursting with excitement when she called me earlier in the day and asked me to meet her at the coffee house that afternoon. I got there about ten minutes early, ordered my favorite drink and sat in "our" booth to wait. I was flipping through my smartphone when she ran in.

She didn't say hi, but just began dragging me out of the booth. "You have to see this." She nearly gushed. She then dragged me to the door and outside.

I stood in the middle of the sidewalk, but I didn't know what I was supposed to see.

"It's right there in front of you," she said, not in the least taking offense at my "blindness."

"All I see in front of me is this cool-looking red . . ." I paused a beat, looked at her and exclaimed, "That's your car?"

"Absolutely," she said, "I got a great deal, but better yet, the lowest interest rate I've paid in years."

She looked as if she were about to cry. "Come on," she said, "I want to take you for a ride. After all, I never could have bought it without your coaching."

As you continue to do the work laid out in this book and follow up on the actions you've taken so far, you'll be cruising around town in a new car with "the lowest interest rate" you've paid in years.
Once you've completed your attack on your credit score, you'll find that you can breathe easier – and perhaps not worry that the next call will someone badgering you to pay your debt.

And the approach outlined in this book, well, it couldn't get much more logical or easier. It just takes a bit of time and discipline on your part.

Just as a reminder and a wrap-up, here are the steps you'll be taking as you delve more and more into your credit repair.

7 STEP CHECKLIST

1. Make up your mind you're ready to improve your credit.

2. Evaluate your past to determine what got you into the credit valley you're currently in.

3. Order a free copy of your credit report and your score.

4. Review the items on your report, paying extra attention to any errors or inaccuracies.

5. Send the credit bureau one letter for each error you discover.

6. Send the provider, the company which furnished the inaccurate information to the credit bureau a dispute letter as well.

7. While you're waiting for a response, take positive action on improving your credit now. Don't take out any loans or open any credit

cards until you're sure you can handle these responsibly.

That's it in a nutshell.

And remember, your credit score is not a number chiseled in stone. Rather, it's a snapshot of where you are right now.

LAST WORDS

I wanted to thank you for buying my book; I am neither a professional writer nor an author, but rather a person who suffered a great deal from bad credit syndrome, and finally decided to take it head on and fix everything. In this book, I wanted to share my knowledge with you, as I know there are many people who share the same passion and drive as I do. So, this book is entirely dedicated to you.

Despite my best effort to make this book error free, if you happen to find any errors, I want to ask for your forgiveness ahead of time.

Just remember, my writing skills may not be best, but the knowledge I share here is pure and honest.

If you thought I added some value and shared some valuable information that you can use, please take a minute and post a review on wherever you bought this book from. This will mean the world to me. Thank you so much!!

Lastly, I wanted to thank my dear friend Elise for all her help and support throughout this book, without them, this book would not have been possible.

Enjoy your new financial freedom.